T0011497 ip

The Office of the President

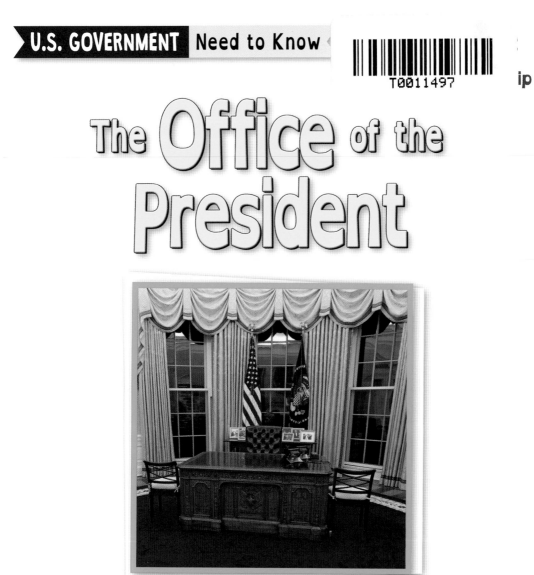

by Karen Latchana Kenney

Consultant: John Coleman
Professor of Political Science, University of Minnesota
Minneapolis, Minnesota

BEARPORT
PUBLISHING

Minneapolis, Minnesota

President: Jen Jenson
Director of Product Development: Spencer Brinker
Senior Editor: Allison Juda
Associate Editor: Charly Haley
Senior Designer: Colin O'Dea

Library of Congress Cataloging-in-Publication Data

Names: Kenney, Karen Latchana, author.
Title: The Office of the President / by Karen Latchana Kenney.
Description: Silvertip Books. | Minneapolis, Minnesota : Bearport
  Publishing Company, [2022] | Series: U.S. Government: Need to Know |
  Includes bibliographical references and index.
Identifiers: LCCN 2021039158 (print) | LCCN 2021039159 (ebook) | ISBN
  9781636916002 (Library Binding) | ISBN 9781636916071 (Paperback) | ISBN
  9781636916149 (eBook)
Subjects: LCSH: Presidents–United States. | Executive departments–United
  States. | Public administration–United States. | United
  States–Politics and government.
Classification: LCC JK516 .K375 2022 (print) | LCC JK516 (ebook) | DDC
  352.230973–dc23
LC record available at https://lccn.loc.gov/2021039158
LC ebook record available at https://lccn.loc.gov/2021039159

For more information, write to Bearport Publishing, 5357 Penn Avenue South, Minneapolis, MN 55419. Printed in the United States of America.

Contents

Leading the Nation

Every four years, the president raises their hand. They promise to do their best for the country. All of our presidents have spoken the same words. As a leader, the president will " . . . **preserve**, protect, and defend the **Constitution** of the United States."

The president's promise is written into the Constitution. It is only 35 words long. This speech is called the oath of office.

President Joe Biden
taking the oath of office

A New Kind of Leader

When the United States was formed, many places were ruled by one leader. It was helpful to have someone at the top. But the country's founders didn't want anyone to have too much power. They decided to have a president. But this person would be only part of the government.

There are three branches, or parts, of our government. The executive branch is led by the president. There is also the legislative branch. This part makes laws. The judicial branch decides the meanings of laws.

The founders made a completely new kind of government.

Presidential Powers

The president is the head of state. This means they speak for everyone from the United States. They are also the head of government. As the leader of the executive branch, they keep the **federal** government running. They make sure laws are carried out.

Part of the president's job as head of state is to meet with leaders from other countries. They are the face of the nation to the rest of the world.

Barack Obama *(right)* met with Russia's president, Vladimir Putin *(left)*, when Obama was president.

Another big job for the president is to lead the United States military. As **commander**-in-chief the president is head of the armed forces. They are in charge of protecting the United States. The president gets help from top members of the military to be sure this is done.

The president's powers with the military are limited. Only the legislative branch can send the country into war. But then the president is in charge of the troops.

11

Check Out the Balance

Just as the founders wanted, the president shares power with others in government. The president gets a say over laws made by the legislative branch. They can even **veto**, or reject, new laws.

The president has some power over the judicial branch, too. They say who should be judges.

The system of spreading out power is called checks and balances. A veto is a check. But, if enough of the legislative branch agrees, they can pass a law the president vetoes. Power is balanced.

The president signs all laws to make them official.

The People behind the President

The president has a lot of power and responsibility. But they do not work alone. The vice president is second in charge after the president. They help the president run the government. The vice president takes over if the president dies, leaves office, or gets very sick.

The vice president's main job is to lead the Senate. Sometimes the Senate has a tie when they vote to make laws. If this happens, the vice president breaks the tie.

Kamala Harris was the first female vice president.

More people help the president, too. Along with the vice president, they make up the president's **cabinet**. Each person in the cabinet is in charge of a different area of the government.

The president picks cabinet members. Then, the Senate gets to approve people for the jobs.

The president's cabinet has 16 people. One leads decisions about education. Another helps with the country's workers. There is even someone in charge of taking care of people who served in the military.

Joe Biden chose Deb Haaland *(top)* and Lloyd J. Austin III *(bottom)* as part of his cabinet.

Job Requirements

Who can become president? The Constitution has three rules about it. A president must have been born in the United States. They have to be 35 or older. And they need to live in the United States for 14 years before an election.

Before taking the top job in the land, some presidents were military leaders. Others were vice presidents or governors. A few were cabinet members or teachers.

John Adams was
a teacher and vice
president before
he was president.

Electing the President

There are elections for the president every four years. The Tuesday after the first Monday in November is Election Day. Citizens who are 18 or older can vote for the president. Their votes come together to make the popular vote.

A president is voted into the job for four years. This is called a term. A 1951 rule says presidents can serve two terms. But before then, President Franklin D. Roosevelt was elected four times.

After Election Day, a small group of people called **electors** vote. Electors stand in for the people from their state. They have the electoral vote. In most places, the person who wins the most votes in that state gets the electoral votes. The winner of this vote becomes president.

Sometimes the person who wins the popular vote does not win the electoral vote. This has happened five times.

An elector voting

23

Where Can You Find the President?

The president works and lives in the same building. This famous building is named the White House. The president's office, called the Oval Office, is in the west side of the building. The president and their family lives in the center of the White House.

The country's first president never lived in the White House. That's because the building wasn't around yet. Second president, John Adams, moved into the White House in 1800.

The White House is in Washington, D.C.

A Position of Power

The president of the United States is one of the most powerful people in the world. But this power comes with a lot of responsibility. Their choices impact hundreds of millions of people. The president serves the people of the country.

What does the future of the presidency look like? Some want to change how we vote for the president. They suggest we pick the president by the popular vote.

The Branches of Government

Legislative Branch	Executive Branch	Judicial Branch
Makes laws Made up of the Senate and the House of Representatives	**Carries out laws** Made up of the president and their office	**Says if laws are followed correctly** Made up of the Supreme Court and other federal courts

The office of the president

The president serves for four years at a time. They get to pick who they lead the country with. This includes the vice president and others in the president's cabinet.

★ SilverTips for REVIEW

Review what you've learned. Use the text to help you.

Define key terms

cabinet

electoral vote

executive branch

head of government

head of state

Check for understanding

What are the president's roles as head of state and head of government? What is their responsibility as the commander-in-chief?

Describe how the president is elected.

What is the president's cabinet? Name at least one job in the cabinet.

Think deeper

How does the president have an impact on your life? Give at least one example.

★ SilverTips on TEST-TAKING

★ **Make a study plan.** Ask your teacher what the test is going to cover. Then, set aside time to study a little bit every day.

★ **Read all the questions carefully.** Be sure you know what is being asked.

★ **Skip any questions** you don't know how to answer right away. Mark them and come back later if you have time.

Glossary

cabinet a group of people who give advice to the leader of a government

commander the person in charge of a military group

Constitution a statement of basic laws and principles for governing a nation, state, or organization

electors people who vote to choose the president

executive related to the branch of a government that includes the president and vice president

federal having to do with the government of a nation

judicial related to the branch of government that includes courts and judges

legislative related to the branch of government with people who make laws

preserve to protect

veto the power of a person to decide that something will not be approved

Read More

Collison, Campbell. *The Presidents (X-Treme Facts: U.S. History).* Minneapolis: Bearport Publishing Company, 2021.

Kellaher, Karen. *The Presidency (A True Book. Why It Matters).* New York: Children's Press, 2020.

Uhl, Xian M. *Electing a U.S. President (Rosen Verified: U.S. Government).* New York: Rosen Publishing, 2021.

Learn More Online

1. Go to **www.factsurfer.com** or scan the QR code below.

2. Enter "**Office of President**" into the search box.

3. Click on the cover of this book to see a list of websites.

Index

About the Author

Karen Latchana Kenney is an author and editor. She lives in Minnetonka, MN.